A Funny Garden

by Rowan Obach

illustrated by
Luciana Navarro Alves

PEARSON
Scott Foresman

Editorial Offices: Glenview, Illinois • Parsippany, New Jersey • New York, New York
Sales Offices: Needham, Massachusetts • Duluth, Georgia • Glenview, Illinois
Coppell, Texas • Ontario, California • Mesa, Arizona

Every effort has been made to secure permission and provide appropriate credit for photographic material. The publisher deeply regrets any omission and pledges to correct errors called to its attention in subsequent editions.

Unless otherwise acknowledged, all photographs are the property of Scott Foresman, a division of Pearson Education.

Photo locators denoted as follows: Top (T), Center (C), Bottom (B), Left (L), Right (R), Background (Bkgd)

Illustrations by Luciana Navarro Alves

ISBN: 0-328-13188-1

9 10 VO54 14 13 12 11 10 09

One day Miss Jones read a book about plants and gardens to her class.

"Can we plant a silly garden?" asked Tom.

"Yes!" said Miss Jones. "We can!"

"What will you plant, Tom?" asked Miss Jones.

"I'll plant my zebra," said Tom.

Miss Jones smiled. "I'm afraid that will not grow. But we can try."

"What will you plant, Lin?" asked Miss Jones.

"I'll plant my trumpet," said Lin.

Miss Jones smiled again. "I'm afraid that will not grow. But we can try."

"I'm going to plant my bells," said Jane.

"I'm going to plant some shoes," said Marc.

"You have picked some funny things to plant," said Miss Jones. "But we can try."

The next day, the class went outside.

"We can make the garden here," said Miss Jones.

Soon the class was busy digging. They dug holes in the hard dirt. They planted the zebra and the trumpet and the bells and the shoes.

In a few weeks, things started to grow.

Miss Jones looked out at the yard. "Oh, my! Class, come and see the garden!" she said.

The class ran into the yard.
"Look at my zebra grass!" shouted Tom.
"Here is my trumpet vine!" yelled Lin.
"See my bell flowers?" asked Jane.
"I have a shoe tree!" shouted Marc.

Miss Jones looked at the garden.

"How did these plants grow?" she asked. "Class, you have planted a funny garden!"

How a Plant Grows

Read Together

A plant starts out as a tiny seed. The seed is planted in soil. The seed needs water and sunlight to grow. Soon the seed will grow roots below the ground. A stem will push up through the soil. As the stem grows taller, leaves will appear. The plant may grow flowers too. Inside each flower new seeds grow. These seeds might make new plants.